THE HALFWAY HOUSE FOR WRITERS

A LIFE IN 10 MINUTES HANDBOOK

Turn your shit into gold!

Valley Haggard

Dedication

This handbook was written for my brave and beautiful students as a companion piece to my classes but I hope it will serve as a respite for wounded writers everywhere.

Thank you

Thank you to Stan and Henry for accepting and loving me for richer and poorer, in sickness and in health, through good times and fights about fried chicken; my parents for their wisdom, humor and lifelong dedication to art; my teachers, students and fellow writers for helping create a writing world I actually want to inhabit.

Thank you to Sarah Allen-Short for her big picture and detail-oriented organizing mind, Anne Carle Carson for her insight and copy editing, Bird Cox for her vision and design and Rob Collins for his technical mastery, wizardry and undying patience.

Cover: "The Valley"
by Mary Chiaramonte, 2013

merrysee.com

I am obsessed with both snakes and rabbits. They represent danger and safety, sides of myself and the creative process that I have been coming to terms with since consciously deciding to take creative rather than destructive risks. Snakes have literally crossed my path during some of the most auspicious occasions of my life: on my wedding day, during my pregnancy with my son, throughout the year my dad became ill. Facing the primal fear I feel in their presence has helped me face some of the darkest, most frightening parts of myself. But snakes haven't been the only creature to show themselves to me again and again. Bunny rabbits began to make an almost daily appearance in my life, neighborhood and backyard when I first began teaching classes for kids and adults. I also have a primal, unbidden reaction each time I see a rabbit: joy. They freeze or dart away, activating a fiercely protective side of myself. I have begun to collect snake and bunny imagery, art and jewelry. From what I've read, snakes represent rebirth and rabbits signify creativity, intuition, paradox, fear and good fortune. I'll take it all, as these are invaluable tools in my kit as a writer. In 2013, I commissioned the amazingly talented Richmond artist Mary Chiaramonte to create a drawing of me with water, mountains and the moon surrounded by bunnies and snakes, my talismans, as I embrace the most frightened, intuitive and powerful sides of myself.

I. Welcome

    Welcome to the Halfway House *1*
    Is This Handbook for You? *3*
    About Me *4*
    Rules of the Halfway House *7*
    For the Writer, Bound and Gagged *13*
    The Ballad of the Wounded Writer *15*

II. The Write Life

    Baby Steps *21*
    Extracting Splinters *23*
    Turn Your Shit Into Gold *25*
    Cheaper Than Therapy *27*
    My Last Dollar *29*
    Sitting on the Edge of the Pool *31*
    Do (and Don't) Trust Yourself *33*
    Triggers *35*
    This Isn't Even a First Draft *37*
    Vehicle *39*
    (Don't Do) What You Think You
          Should Be Doing *41*
    Follow Your Nose *43*
    Get Naked *45*
    Not Just a Head *47*
    Recovery *49*

III. Pen to Page

    Right Now I Am *53*
    Prompts *55*
    Up the Creek without a Prompt
          or Paddle *57*
    Letters *59*

Experiment 61
Sideways 63
Under Construction 65
Running Through the Museum 67
Polyester Patchwork Quilt 69
Snakes on Medusa's Head 71
Writing a Bridge 73
Reasons to Quit 75
Underwhelming Goals 77

IV. My Story
Tell the Truth 81
Humble Pie 83
Live Your Life 85
Publication 87
Writers, Queens and Gods 89
Literary Snobs 92
Service & Work 93
Writing Teacher 96

V. My Writing
When I Was Born 101
Where I'm From 104
Love Was 106
16 Ways to Say I Do 108
I Remember You 111
Pest Control 113
Question in Class:How Did You
*   Stop Hating Yourself? 115*
What, If I Don't Find a Way to Say It,
*   Will Kill Me? 117*

*Passing Notes to Friends
        and Strangers 119*
Halfway House for Writers 121
Competitive Depression 123
Last Night of Writing Class 125
While I Was Gone 127

VI. Life in 10 Minutes
        10 Minutes at a Time 131
        An Invitation 133
        Write Now 135

I. WELCOME

Welcome to the Halfway House

You know everything you need to know.

You have everything you need to have.

Nothing has been wasted: none of your writing and none of your time.

Even lost years and lost manuscripts were necessary to bring you where you are now.

All that's lost can be salvaged.

You bring with you the most sacred and the most profane.

You bring wisdom and humor and a broken, healing heart.

You bring your living body and your limitless soul and enough stories, thoughts and dreams to fill a thousand books.

There is no hurry, there is no pressure, there is no wrong way to do this.

There is no rule book, there is no map save for what's inside of you.

You know now which voices to trust and which to lay gently aside.

There is nothing you have to prove or solve or figure out.

There is no timeline or deadline.

You can trust the words that come.

You can trust yourself.

You were brought here for this.

You were led to this.

This is why you are here.

Welcome home.

Is This Handbook for You?

If you are confident, joyful and productive in your writing life, if you understand your place in the world of writing, if you are happy and carefree when you think of what you have written and what you still want to write, this handbook is not for you.

If you have struggled with insecurity, existential angst, being stuck and feeling unworthy; if you have wrestled with writing that is too crazy, too boring, too shameful, unorganized, or just plain sucks, read on.

This handbook is for writers who are afraid to begin and writers who have begun but are afraid to continue.

This handbook is for anyone haunted by writing, writers who long to write but fear it, writers who are afraid to call themselves writers.

This handbook is the culmination of recurring themes and threads that have arisen in my writing classes again and again and the process by which my students and I have begun to recover from our crippling, debilitating and false beliefs.

This handbook is a guide to rehabilitation for wounded writers.

About Me

I've been brought up by high school literary magazines and college creative writing workshops. I have been a camper, counselor and director of creative writing camps for kids. I have been in writing groups and writing classes. I have interviewed authors and reviewed their books. I have judged fiction contests, fellowships and awards for children and adults. I have taught creative nonfiction workshops, classes and retreats. I have been a book editor, published in anthologies and authored first person columns.

I am in recovery from everything. Alcohol and drugs and money and donuts and love. But also a lifelong addiction to terrorizing myself as a writer, editing myself down to the bone, comparing my writing to everyone else's and basically sacrificing myself at the altar of unrealistic expectations. I have been searching for a process by which to lay down my weapons, to stop holding myself hostage, to stop strangling my work before it has a chance to breathe. I am learning to become a gentle editor and a kind friend to myself on the page.

What follows are some of the most essential things I have learned about writing after studying hundreds of books and teaching hundreds of writers of every level and degree of experience. In this handbook, I have written about some of the most common themes and threads that have arisen repeatedly in my classes, practical advice for getting started on the page, the story of my own journey towards healing as a writer, some samples of my work that have emerged from my practice and an invitation to submit your own writing to my online literary magazine, Life in 10 Minutes.

I am not in charge of the Halfway House — I am a student of it. Every single day when I sit down to write I am a beginner. Whether you have written every day of your life or none, welcome. We are all on the same blank page together.

Rules of the Halfway House

1. *Surrender your weapons.*

We have abused and belittled ourselves long enough. We have been our own worst enemies, our own worst critics, the harshest arbiters on Judgment Day. We have ignored and neglected our writing altogether or shot it down in infant form, before it had the chance to take its first breath. The first rule of the Halfway House is to stop, to arrest our masochistic tendencies and let our work be what it is.

2. *Seek shelter.*

Create structure. Build a frame to contain the vibrant, messy paint of your words. Erect a property line within which the wild animals of your writing can run without being slammed into on the highway. Whether your structure is a timer at your desk, a writing class, a writing group or an accountability partner it helps to have structure within which to create.

As much as you may want to consider yourself a free spirit who writes with wild abandon, the truth is most of us need structure. Otherwise our writing blobs forth like an amoeba, Jello, the inside of the body without any skin. Or, it fails to launch at all. We need a vessel to pour our words into. Create a vessel.

10 minutes at a time is that vessel for me. It holds the beginning of something big or the entirety of something small. It's a poem or a letter, the jumble of thoughts clogging up the brain like leaves and sticks and twigs in a gutter. Ideas lurking in the back of the mind or buried in the heart. The overwhelm of shoulds and to-do lists that could stop me before I even get started. But I do, because 10 minutes gives my thoughts a place to sit while I move on, discovering what lurks beneath.

3. *Free Write.*

I advocate for stream-of-consciousness, unedited, uncensored free-writing. Like Anne Lamott's "shitty first drafts," Julia Cameron's "morning pages" and Natalie Goldberg's "writing practice," write now and edit later. Free-writing is the way in which we bypass writer's block, get our engines revving, shoot past all the buts and can'ts lining the highways of our minds. Free-writing helps us develop our intuition, calls on us to trust ourselves, summons up from our subconscious what wants to be written.

When we are free-writing we throw spelling, grammar and punctuation out the window. We don't try to censor or control ourselves. We begin to make our way back to the playground of writing we inhabited before the teacher/parent/ex/priest/ego/addict tried to kick us out. Free-writing helps us reclaim our own voices, our stories and our right to exist.

4. *Hand write.*

I suggest writing by hand with a pen or pencil in a notebook because it makes it much more difficult to check Facebook or research an obscure reference or decide to delete everything you've just written. Writing by hand is a basic, primal practice that will allow the pace of your hand to regulate the pace of your thoughts. Write your second draft on your keyboard or computer and—if you'd like—edit as you go. But write your first draft by hand.

5. *Skip the small talk.*

If there's an elephant in the room, don't spend too much time describing the wallpaper. You don't need to waste your time or anyone else's pretending everything is fine if it isn't. Writing doesn't have to be a cocktail party where everyone looks glamorous delivering witty one-liners. Get to the meat and potatoes. Don't fill up on candied mints and forfeit the meal. Writing the truth in this way may feel awkward and messy and vulnerable but it's a good way to bypass the fluff and cut out the fat. Readers yearn to connect with the truth. Practicing telling the emotional truth is a good way to write, and to live.

6. *Listen.*

As soon as you are done writing, read your work out loud. Something very different happens when we hear our words spoken than when we write them down. Read aloud to yourself, or to someone else—they don't have to comment, critique or give advice. In fact it may be better if they don't. Often we feel completely differently about a piece when we hear it, almost as if someone else wrote it and read it back to us. Someone we might actually like and treat with respect. I find that people cry, or laugh, or sweat or shake more often when they are reading their work out loud than when they are writing it. It's a good sign. It means you've hit the right vein.

7. *Don't apologize.*

Don't apologize for your work. Don't apologize for being a human being who wrote something down. You don't have to excuse, degrade or mock what you've written. There's no need to explain that the piece in front of you is not perfect, that it might be boring, unfinished, repetitive, shocking, uncomfortable, intimate, TMI, self-indulgent or nonsensical. Practice letting it be what it is. See it as the rendering of a moment in time. It may be full of contradiction or paradox or moaning and groaning or gushing or trying to figure something out. It may read like someone tumbling naked down an avalanche. That's fine. It's a first draft. It's part of a process, not the finished product. Let it be.

For the Writer, Bound and Gagged

(Or the letter I wrote to myself when I woke up one morning at a writer's retreat frozen with fear.)

There is the terror that you won't get your words out, that the images and ideas and thoughts and stories will remain prisoners in your mind and that if they do manage to escape they will be mangled, bleeding, broken.

There is the fear that you are the wrong vessel for this cargo, that you have been accidentally gifted ideas and urges far too magnificent and grand for lowly, earthbound, humanly flawed little you to carry out, even in a million lifetimes.

There is the embarrassment at your own desire, the burning lifelong longing to do this one thing that is forever at the edge of your fingertips, on the tip of your tongue, just a breath out of reach, scared off by the fierceness of your wanting.

There is the free-floating anxiety that you will never be good enough, never be worthy, never live up to the burden of your own expectations.

There is the bond with self-sabotage and self-loathing, the fear of success outweighing even the fear of failure. You have clung to the

Why, then, are we here?

To bear witness to our own lives and to the lives of those around us.

To have something to do when there is nothing that can be done.

To find out with greater clarity what we think, know, feel and believe.

To fight the man.

To give voice to the child who was shushed, silenced, unacknowledged.

To prove that we are here.

To find our connection to humanity.

To find our connection with ourselves.

To speak our truth.

To not let the bastards keep us down.

To write the hardest thing and have someone else say, "me too."

To extract the splinters from our minds, one spear, one sliver at a time.

To heal the wounded, crippled writer, to give ourselves a voice and space to breathe.

II. THE WRITE LIFE

Baby Steps

When the Alaskan cruise ship on which I'd been a stewardess docked in Seattle and I took an Amtrak home to Richmond, my mother referred to the house she was about to rent to me as a halfway house where she was going to help me reclaim the life I'd been hell-bent on wrecking. It was also the house I'd grown up in, the house of my childhood, where she and I had lived until I was 15, while my dad had moved 15 times around town.

In this "halfway house" I quit drinking, smoking and moving from state to state. I beat my couch with a whiffle ball bat, cried my eyes out, learned how to pay rent and felt, at 23, that my life was already over. I couldn't listen to music, go to plays or do anything "cultural." I had to go out and buy records I'd never heard before. I couldn't even read the poetry I loved. Everything made me want to drink. Everything was a trigger.

When I finally was able to write, I wrote big loopy lines of crazed self-pity and despair. But it was a step. An important step. I was emptying my head and heart of the knots of confusion and destruction I'd created inside. I was clearing space for new thoughts, new stories, a new life and new material.

When one of my mother's friends bragged that his son had graduated law school, my mother bragged back that her daughter had gotten sober. It was a low, but important point in my life. At the time however, I didn't think so. I was full of shame and knew myself to be a failure. Mary Shelley wrote Frankenstein when she was 19. I couldn't even look people in the eye in the grocery store but felt I should have already met Oprah, written a literary bestseller, achieved critical acclaim. I didn't recognize what a big deal it was just to buy a notebook and fill it. But it was. It was the beginning of coming home, growing up, seeing the world as it was, seeing myself for who I was.

Be gentle with yourself. The tiny steps you're taking may be bigger than you think.

Extracting Splinters

I think of writing practice as a process of extracting splinters. Whether you extract the biggest splinter or the smallest first doesn't matter. You may choose the shard piercing your foot that cripples you or the tiny thorn in your side. But keep going. Keep extracting splinters, one at a time.

I have written slowly, bit by bit, over time, a series of essays and stories that have exposed me layer by layer—each line, each piece, revealing a little bit more. And with each revelation, each confession, I have accepted myself more fully. As I've uncovered my deepest flaws, I've also uncovered strengths, hidden beneath the festering splinters. Each extracted splinter reveals tender pink flesh eager to heal.

For many years I used a first person column in a monthly women's magazine and my own blog as vehicles for this process. I wrote about myself as a recovering alcoholic and addict, as a teenage bi-sexual, my brush with divorce and bankruptcy, getting sued by two credit card companies, my love affair with food, my online affair, posing naked, being a secret smoker, being raised on food stamps and welfare, moving 15 times with my dad when I was growing up, and that time I let my house get overrun by cockroaches. There is still more to go but each piece I release into the world is one less piece of baggage I have to carry alone. Whether many people read it, or a few, or one or none, I am relieved of the burden of secrecy and shame.

Now each time I sit down to write, I start with an internal mental, emotional, spiritual and physical body scan, seeking out sore spots that, left to fester, will become infected. Wherever there is a splinter still lodged—age old or brand new—I extract it by naming it, by writing it out until it has lost some of its sting, some of its power. Only then can I move on.

The pen is the tweezers, the lance and the sword. It is the surgeon's knife with the power to cut and ultimately, to heal.

Turn Your Shit Into Gold

For most of us, writing is the one true chance at alchemy we will have in this lifetime. Only through writing are we able to take the devastation, shame, disappointment and all-time lows of our lives and turn them into something not only useful to ourselves and others, but beautiful, radiant and powerful.

There is a saying in the writing world: "Bad life equals good writing." And whenever someone shares their deepest pain and saddest stories with me, their tragedies and mistakes—the stuff of death and divorce, addiction and abuse—I say, "Here is your treasure, your gold mine, your most precious material. Use it. Let it work for you."

We may have to get our hands dirty in the process. Entering into our darkness, into the rooms that cast the deepest shadows, doesn't always feel good. But it's how we can begin to reclaim our selves and our lives.

Personally, I have plenty to work with. I have a horizontal 13-inch scar above my right hip where the adrenal gland with the tumor and a rib came out. I have a half-inch scar on my knee from sticking it in a metal fan one summer day when I was 10 and at home alone. I have the scar above my pubic bone where they retrieved my son with the cord triple wrapped around his neck—via cesarean section—and later my uterus, shot through with tumors. Each scar and nick on my body tells a story, but the most enduring scars aren't visible. Addiction, affairs, divorce, food stamps, shame, daddy issues, recovery from self-loathing—this is the bedrock of my material.

Now when I remember something new, something worse, I know that it contains a gift if I am willing to work long enough with the painful raw material. Sometimes I can't write coherently about an issue that's still bleeding until it's begun to heal, to scab over, to become a scar. But I don't think it matters so much when we write about it, so long as we do.

She survived multiple heart surgeries, her son was killed in combat, his house burned down. Turn your shit into gold. These are the stories we look to, to teach us how we would survive them, too.

Cheaper than Therapy

Sometimes people tell me they take my class because it's cheaper than therapy. Though I've fought it for years, it's actually true that writing can be therapy. When we write without crossing out every word we say, we are healing our wounded writers and by proxy our wounded selves. We are not therapists—at least most of us aren't—but we are each our own patients capable of writing our way through and towards some kind of healing. As we write and create our stories, aspects of ourselves come together in a new way like connective tissue over a wound. I have hated God and known for a fact that God hated me. My body has been cut open and stitched back together. I've lost babies and boyfriends and dear friends. I've been the heartbreaker and the heartbroken, second best, invisible and right up front, out loud.

Each story I write about the lives I've experienced and the lives I've witnessed has been a bandage, gauze, brace, staples and stitches until I could walk on my own again. We come with big and little sorrow, great and simple joy. We drag ourselves through the mud and recite prayer on mountaintops. We answer our own questions. We ask questions we didn't even know we wanted answers to. This isn't an hour on the couch—it's flight straight through to the interior. There's no one to tell us what to do next in our marriages or with our children or our careers or our homes or our next meals. But we can look at what we have and where we've come from and decide to claim it or change it or accept it or heal it. We can say "this is my voice speaking my truth at least for this moment and it may be universal or unique, it may be unacceptable or rude, it may not be polite dinner conversation but it is what I've pulled up from inside that can sustain me." I guess it is cheaper than therapy: a notebook, a pen, courage and guts.

My Last Dollar

After I was laid off from my desk job with benefits, when my husband was starting up his own business and before I could support myself teaching, I was broke all the time. Every month I juggled the bills, leaving many unopened in my desk drawer hoping they would magically disappear. We didn't have health insurance. Sometimes utilities got shut off. There were a lot of rice and beans. If I went out for coffee, I'd bemoan spending my last dollar.

I spent my last dollar so many times I finally figured out it wasn't my last dollar. They kept coming. Not as many as I would have liked as quickly as I would have liked, but I never had to sleep on the streets. We never missed a meal. Just when I felt that all was lost, another dollar would appear.

The same is true with writing. Sometimes we are convinced we have used up all of our material. We have nothing left. We are dried up empty shells, exoskeletons. The bug has left the body. But if we can sit down, setting our expectations, demands and horror aside, the next word will come. A new phrase or thought. Perhaps we are presented with a different way of entering old material. In this case, beggars can't be choosers. Don't dismiss what comes as too small or insignificant. It will lead you to the next thought until the small trickle becomes more like a flood.

Sitting on the Edge of the Pool

Push gently against your comfort zone—feel out the edge and then give the tiniest little push. You do not have to burst that bubble, to reveal all of yourself at once. You don't have to smear the guts of your insides all over your outsides the very first time you sit down to write.

I think of easing into the writing process as putting one toe into the shallow end of the pool and then getting your ankles wet and then your thighs, rather than belly flopping off the high dive—although you can try that, too. The only goal is to end up in the pool eventually, allowing yourself to be bathed and baptized in the full experience of water. Then you can use all of your muscles, ignite all of your nerve endings, alive and awakened. But you don't have to get there all at once. It only matters that you don't spend your entire day sitting on the edge of the pool longing to swim.

When it's time to tell the story of how you wrecked your life or lost your marriage, how your husband had a sex change, how your wife left you or your best friend died, your addictions or secrets, you can do it at your own pace. But I think it's best that you do it. When I hear stories like these in my classes it is always an honor. It is never a burden—it is always a gift. I feel deeply trusted, that I have been given a glimpse into the sacred.

Sometimes writers hold back, apologize. They want their lives to be shinier, prettier, less messy. But the reader wants to feel that you are real, human, fallible. The reader wants your honesty and your guts. You don't have to do a full monty strip-tease right away. You can remove just one bobby pin in order to begin.

Do (and Don't) Trust Yourself

You are simultaneously right and wrong. You both know and you don't know. Half of you trusts yourself to move forward, to tell the truth, and the other half is screaming at you to shut up, to be quiet, to keep your head down. Don't make noise or draw attention! Writers have many voices going in their heads at all times and these two—the devil and the angel voice—tend to be the loudest. The voice rising up from deep inside yourself that wants you to tell your story, and the voice that wants you— and your writing—dead. Buried, silenced and underground.

One voice will lead you through the magical door of your dreams, the other to a pit deep in hell that looks a lot like watching cable on the couch eating an entire bag of cheese puffs. It seems like distinguishing between these two voices should be easy. But it isn't. Somehow both voices manage to sound equally convincing, equally like the omniscient, all powerful, all knowing voice of God. How do we know which voice to trust and which to send back to the hell from whence it came?

We can start by putting them both on the page. We can ask for an outside opinion, one that's a little more objective than our own. We can wait 24 hours and see if we can think a little more clearly. 99.9% of the time the voice that tells us to shut up, quit writing and devour a dozen frosted donuts and a box of pink wine isn't the voice we should be listening to.

Triggers

We all have our blind spots. We all have our Achilles Heel. Like addicts and alcoholics, writers have triggers. But instead of making us drink, our triggers stall our pens on the page. As we describe the twists and turns and details of our lives, we think, "Oh God, this is boring (or sentimental or ridiculous or self-indulgent or pretentious or bad or crazy or hokey or stupid or whorish or dumb)."

Our triggers are tough, sneaky and subtle. They have come from past criticisms that have created wounds—both from inside and outside of ourselves. But just because we are triggered doesn't mean we have to stop writing.

In fact, writing about our triggers when they come up is excellent material. What does boring really mean? Does it mean that you are afraid nobody else cares what you think, who you are, how you spend your day? Does it mean you think everyone else's alcoholic father was more interesting than yours? That your heartache doesn't count because you weren't dumped by a movie star or a vampire? Maybe you think you are pretentious when you write what you know or self-indulgent when, even once, you talk about yourself.

Turning your triggers into prompts will help

unearth deeper truths, the stories beneath the stories. Use them to your advantage, turn them into fuel to go deeper, rather than as an excuse to quit writing.

This Isn't Even a First Draft

I have had a writing mentor read my best effort, scoff and say, "This isn't even a first draft." I have had editors rewrite every word of my stories. I have had the personal essays I've worked hardest on sent back for revision or rejected outright. One guy even said, "I'm tired of making change for your two dollar metaphors that should only cost me a dime." I've received praise and compliments too, but those are harder to remember.

Unfortunately, the most damning critic of all has been myself. Once, a friend suggested that I was a perfectionist, though I didn't see how that could be possible if nothing I wrote was perfect. Now I understand that that was her point precisely. Perfectionism is a sneaky and insidious form of insanity. There's a phrase I've heard in recovery circles: *Go where the love is.* That has become my motto in the writing world, too. Find people who support your writing. But most importantly, learn how to support your own writing. Describe your inner critic and see if he/she/it resembles anyone you know. Mine looks a lot like an amalgamation of some particularly nasty ex-boyfriends. Figuring that out helped remove some of my internal critic's power.

This doesn't mean I think every scribble is

precious or that there's no room for improvement, but even the worst crap I come up with moves me along in my writing. Just as fertilizer isn't the bounty we hope to serve at our table, it is still an integral part of the growing process. A social worker friend observed that I give "strength based feedback." It is not a stretch for me to find something I like, something beautiful or profound, something worthy of expansion in every piece of writing I read or hear, even from the greenest of beginners. Giving positive, gentle feedback comes naturally and easily for me, though I am still in the process of learning to give it in a regular way to myself. At the very least I know that even work in the fertilizer stage is at least a first draft.

Vehicle

Writing can change the way you feel, the way you see the world, the things you notice. It won't (necessarily) make you rich or skinny or famous or better equipped to organize your Tupperware drawer; but it will light up your insides and, over time, give you a sense of belonging in both the world and your body.

Writing is a vehicle for exploring, communicating, storytelling, connecting, making sense of the nonsensical, the overwhelming, the beautiful, the tragic. Writing is a vehicle; it is not the destination where you hope one day to arrive.

As a new book reviewer, desperate to publish anything at all, to at last "arrive" in the world of writing, I interviewed an author with two PhDs who had published one critically acclaimed book, had another one on the way and was a regular contributor to the *New York Times*. I hoped I could—by osmosis—catch what she had, that she could show me the "way," help me get "there" (wherever "there" was), indoctrinate me into the cult of the well-published so I could at last breathe easy.

"I feel like such a failure," she told me as our interview got underway. "At my age, I've only written two books. I'm not as accomplished as

X, Y or Z." And in that moment I got it. There would always be further to go, more to accomplish. I could be a happy and fulfilled unknown writer or a miserable bestseller. There was no direct correlation between publication and everlasting inner peace.

Another author friend of mine drove the point home. "Hurry up and get your book published, Valley," he said, "so you can be unhappy with the rest of us." There is nothing wrong with publication or success, but it has little to do with the writing life we choose to experience in the meantime.

(Don't Do) What You Think
You Should Be Doing

Do what you are doing instead of what you think you should be doing. Write what you want to write instead of what you think you *should* want to write. This may sound obvious but most of us think we should follow a script or prescription that will eventually equate to turning us into "real writers." It's good to know the different forms that are available, but if they squeeze the life out of you and your writing, try something else.

Maybe you like writing lists. Lists of ex-lovers or ingredients for Mexican hot chocolate or strangers you've seen on trains in other countries. Maybe you like to write eulogies or prose poems or letters to the dead or to people who haven't been born yet or that you've never met before. Maybe you like to write all dialogue with no description or you love to describe landscapes and interiors, lush or arid, cramped or expansive. Maybe you only want to write about emotions—rage, bliss, sorrow, longing, confusion, joy—and the stories that shaped you as you embodied those feelings. Write what draws you in, what moves you, what interests you, not what you think will interest someone else.

I have always loved the short form, flash

fiction, slice of life. But I thought I should write a novel. Real writers write novels. I spent two years writing a novel. I set deadlines for myself. I wrote my novel on retreats and in classes and at my desk at 5:00 a.m. I agonized and groaned and beat my chest over my novel. And then one spring in the bath I had an Aha/Duh moment. How about writing what I actually have been writing, instead of what I think I should have been writing? I asked myself. What about the 10-minute pieces that have accumulated in 25+ journals over five years of teaching creative nonfiction classes?

And in that Aha/Duh moment, the idea for my online literary magazine and my manuscript, Life in 10 Minutes, was born.

Follow Your Nose

I have paid my dues writing ad copy, product descriptions and tedious calendar updates. Being given the freedom to write my own column for a monthly women's magazine was a gift, but to come up with regular subject material, I had to learn to follow my nose.

Since I felt so broken, I decided to experience a different alternative healing modality each month, becoming my own self-improvement guinea pig. I meditated at the Buddhist temple and had my house feng shui-ed. After both visits the feng shui consultant told us our only hope was to move, a suggestion we never managed to take. I danced the 5 Rhythms, dipped my toe in the waters of Continuum, or what the teacher called "yoga on acid," visited past lives with Rohun. The rabbi who studied Kabbalah and channeled a being from another dimension told me not to get the corporate job with benefits and stay on my path as a writer. The astrologer suggested I adopt a regular writing schedule and use a bold voice while the Tarot card reader demanded I stop leaking my energy through dead-end volunteer jobs that were bleeding me dry. I got something interesting and vital from each experience but after a few years in this vein, I felt the answers I was seeking might be found closer to home.

I started another column, "Almost Alternative: Navigating the Fine Line Between the Bohemian and the Bourgeois," about my life as a mother, a wife, a self-employed writer. I wrote about the lessons I learned waiting tables at Waffle House, how my self-employed artist mom had been an example of survival to me, our grief over the death of our beloved dog, being a terrible housekeeper while vowing to stop apologizing for our house.

Each article has been a brick in the foundation I've been building in the world of creative nonfiction, first person narrative. Write what you want to know. Follow your nose and write your way home.

Get Naked

A number of years ago, at a vision board making party at a friend's apartment in the Fan, I glued a magazine photo of a naked goddess statue onto my rectangle of white poster board. Directly across the coffee table from me was local artist Susan Singer cutting out the words "gallery show." I had recently been invited to participate in the Artists and Writers collaborative show at Randolph Macon College, but the first artist I'd asked had said, "OK. You write the words and I'll paint over them." This was not exactly what I had in mind. Susan painted nude women of all sizes and shapes and in that moment I knew I had found my partner. The only hitch was the abject terror I felt at the whole idea. Taking my clothing off for an artist I barely knew—let alone being painted and hung on display in a gallery—was the most frightening idea I'd had in a long time. I knew I had to do it.

I kept track of my thoughts, impressions and feelings as I posed for the photo shoot, as I saw the photographs, drawings and paintings she created, as the art was prepared to be hung for the show. But the most profound part of this experience was twofold. Not only did I experience being painted and seen naked, Susan suggested I share my unedited thoughts as well. I typed them up as they were, and they hung as naked as I was next to the pictures of my bare flesh, rolls, creases, curves, the mountains and valleys of me. It was a terrifying, liberating experience. And a big turning point.

Looking at my body and my words without clothes or edits was a shock that jolted me awake to a more real, a more authentic vision of myself as a writer and a human being.

Not Just a Head

For most of my life I've felt like a floating head that just happened to come attached to a body. And my body was something I wanted to avoid by any means necessary. Escape was the magic word. I used whatever substance, person, liquid or solid to escape feeling how I felt. Writers need only sit in a dark room with a bottle, a cigarette and a leather-bound book to be writers. Moving between my couch, bed and chair was movement enough for me. Re-entering my body through activity and exercise has been a revelation of just the last few years. I have begun to crave the cultivation of the body, mind, spirit connection.

Getting out of my head helps me make better use of the time I spend in it. Group fitness classes at the gym were a great beginning vehicle. Like writing class, they demanded my attention and gave me structure. Learning how to cook, tending to my home and yard, practicing yoga and running with my dog have all had a profound and positive impact on my writing life. I take yoga classes from one of my students, and she takes writing classes from me. We have taught a workshop that combines yoga, writing and meditation 10 minutes at a time that has been pure bliss to experience.

In the mornings my hound dog and I take a

slow, sweaty two-mile run down to the creek with the owls and past the stretch of bamboo. We look for the crows who caw at us and the bunnies that dart by into the brambles. I chew on questions and road bumps in my writing, allowing the thoughts to form momentum with my feet. As I wake up to my body, I have better access to the writing that has been forming inside of it.

Recovery

Recovery in the Halfway House might look like joining a writing group, taking a class or finding an accountability partner to read your work. It might look like spending 10 minutes a week writing, pushing through to the finish line of your novel or signing up for a poetry slam. It might mean joining an ARTS Anonymous meeting or committing to the process of Julia Cameron's *The Artist's Way*, alone or in a group. It might mean that you are more gentle with yourself as you write or that you allow yourself to write at all. It might mean filling in the word "writer" in the blank next to occupation:_____.

Recovery might mean creating a regular writing routine or loosening up the constricting routine you already have. It might mean changing your definition of discipline, editing or what constitutes acceptable writing. It might mean identifying your triggers and stripping them of their power. I think recovery is an ongoing process that looks different for everyone. Every time I call my sponsor with the next painful situation she says, "It's coming up for healing," and most of the time now I see whatever I've called about as a new source of material rather than the end of the road. I have tried to take advantage of every healing balm I can get my hands on. I've needed all the help I could get.

It's becoming simpler as I follow the rules: laying down my weapons, seeking shelter, skipping the small talk, learning to listen, letting my work be. This morning as I ran through the fog of the mountains a bunny hopped across my path. I panted up the steep hills towards the river and thought about how I've come to love the curves of my belly, the rolls of my thighs, my writing process just as it is, right here, unfolding from the middle. And right now that is progress for me.

III. PEN TO PAGE

Right Now I Am

When you have a blank page, start with the words "Right Now I Am." At the beginning of every creative nonfiction class I teach, this is how we start. We write for 10 minutes, nonstop, until the timer goes off. "Right Now I Am" is our imperial and holy dumping ground.

We slough off the week, the day, the hour before, when we couldn't find parking, when we fought with our mothers, when our hearts broke again, when we heard the song on the radio that made us think of home. We write to get current, to get centered, to arrive. We write to process our day and our week, as a chance to see what we're thinking and feeling so we can move forward with what we want and leave the rest behind. We use this 10 minutes as a fireman's hose, cleaning out the crowded gutters of our thoughts, packed in tight with dirt and twigs and sticks and the abandoned mobile homes of birds who've long since moved out.

We empty our minds onto the page and in so doing, generate the prompts for what we will write about next. I believe that if we follow the present moment backwards far enough on gossamer strings of thought we find ourselves connected to the entire web of our mind and memories, the subjects and stories that have been waiting for us to suss them out.

Sometimes we write gorgeous perfectly timed essays that tie up succinctly with a bow when the timer goes off. But that's not usually the case. Usually we come up with a raw, messy, incoherent string of unconnected thoughts that miraculously give way to what we didn't even know we were thinking, what we didn't even know we needed to uncover. Sometimes this leads to poems or short stories or blog posts or the beginnings of memoirs or novels. Sometimes it's just about the process, the holy act of slowing down enough to move our hands across the page.

Prompts

Prompts are everywhere all around you, all the time. If you have recently been startled awake from a dream, taken a bite out of an apple, crossed a busy intersection or lived another day, you have new material to draw from.

If you want to draw from the past rather than the present, firsts are fertile ground. First apartment, first kiss, first time leaving your hometown or state, first motorcycle ride, first funeral, first drink, first friend, first breakup, first boy-girl party, first prayer, first revelation.

And lasts. The last lie you told, the last action you regret, the last thing you gave away for free, the last time you betrayed yourself, the last time you fell in love, the last idol you worshipped, the last time you drove away from a job you loved.

I'm also a big fan of turning points, decisions, hinges, the crux of the moment. Why did you say no even as she tried to put the ring on your finger or move cross country, sight unseen? Why did you choose this college or spouse or state instead of another? What if you hadn't shown up on the day that changed your life? What happened when you did?

Maps are also packed with story. Every house/

apartment/yurt/condo/hotel/tent you've ever lived in, each job you've ever worked, each car you've driven, each person you've dated, each person you wanted to date but didn't.

Dig into the losses and disappointments and also—what went surprisingly well? What miracles have befallen you, what unexpected grace have you endured? A list of what you want to write about and a list of what you don't want to write about ever in a million years is sure to get you somewhere. And what of people? Write for 10 minutes about each family member, priest, friend, ex, rabbi, coach, student or enemy you've ever known.

How about a detailed list of things you remember and things you don't? Write a list of the things you know and the things you don't. Write about where you've come from and where you've ended up. That's sure to keep you busy for a while.

Up the Creek Without a Prompt or a Paddle

Though we are surrounded by prompts and memories and people and experiences, sometimes we flail and flounder trying to get a handle on what to actually write. Sometimes we have no clue what's coming next.

Sometimes we try to set sail without a paddle. We stop and start and circle back on ourselves. We don't always have the luxury of a prompt or know exactly what we need to say or where to start. It feels like quicksand, like mud. I picture that big, round vortex machine at the science museum that you drop your penny in and it circles round and round before finally dropping down, deep into the well at its center. We may feel we have lost our way, that we're veering around wildly.

But then suddenly, if we've kept at it, we find our groove. We are sucked into a place we didn't even know we needed to go, a place that no one else can discover for us, a place that feels oddly like home. This is why I've veered away from giving prompts in writing classes, or if I do, why they are so open-ended. I believe our material, what we are meant to write about, will rise up out of our subconscious, like a body from the bottom of a lake, if we let it. If we are not waiting, pen in hand, treading water, we will miss it.

We have to be willing to start, not knowing in advance what will come. We can't outline or impose order on the wild interior of our writing worlds through pre-planned, advanced directives. We have to learn to get comfortable sitting in the awkward discomfort of not knowing. We tread water with our pen until we see our island or our fish or our mermaid or our buried treasure and then we are ready at last to swim.

I never plan anymore what I will write before I sit down to do it. I don't get very far thinking about writing; I have to actually write. I don't always meet my own material with grace or beauty, but I try not to send it away and let it drown when it comes.

Letters

Write a letter to yourself. Write a letter to yourself when you were a child, or as the old person you imagine you will one day be. Write a letter to someone in which you say everything you can't actually say. Let it rip. Let it all hang out. Cuss a blue streak. Tell that person all of the horrible things they did wrong. Write a letter you know you will shred or burn. Write a letter of thanks to God. Write a letter of condemnation to God. Write a letter to your parents, dead or living. Write a letter to your ancestors. Write a letter to your future children or your current children. Write a letter to your higher self or your lower self or your angels. Write a letter to your childhood, to the houses you used to live in, to winter, to your dog.

I use a "Dreaded Letter" exercise frequently with my teenaged students, and they love it. They love the catharsis and empowerment of giving voice to what they cannot say. It is satisfying to shred or burn or ball up those words when you're done with them, to watch them disappear. Writing is a powerful form of communication whether it is ever read by anyone else or not. Writing is a dialogue with yourself. It is being with who you are, how you are.

Write to process what is going on with you in

this moment and to share that process with someone else. Mine your letters for lines and phrases, hot words and thoughts. Mail them out or keep them home and shape them into a story or a poem.

Experiment

As you put your raw materials down on the page, you might experiment with tense and point of view. If you are writing a piece that feels too personal, too close, too intimate and painful, if it's hard for you to see what you're writing clearly, try writing your story in the third person. Use "she" or "he" as the protagonist rather than "I" or "me." *She held her hands to her belly, refusing to believe that the doctor was unable to find a heartbeat in the invisible ocean inside of her.*

Sometimes pulling out of the frame in this way helps us focus, see the bigger picture and experience the story outside of our own limited perspective. On the other hand, if you want more intimacy with your reader, if you want to invite them to experience the story for themselves, try the second person, "you." *As you walk into his house and are enveloped in the sense that he is more of a stranger than a friend, you wrap your arms protectively around your chest as if you can create armor out of flesh.*

If you want your story to feel more immediate, try writing in the present tense, allowing every detail and twist to unfold right now as you're writing, in real time. *We collapse breathless on our bellies and rub our scraped and bloody knees together right there on the ground in the*

*park because though we are friends, we want to
be sisters, blood sisters bound forever in time.*

It's a good practice to experiment with the tools
of tense and point of view. They can help
change the atmosphere, mood and direction of
the story you're telling. Try telling the story
from the perspective of one of the characters
you are writing about. Write about what it was
like to raise you from the perspective of your
father, or the day of your birth in the voice of
your mother. Can you write memories from
your childhood as if you were once again a
child? Even a subtle change in perspective and
point of view can create big changes in how you
see—and write—your own stories.

Sideways

I think of the world of writing as a big house with many rooms, hiding places, a big attic packed with boxes, a basement, a house with many windows and many doors. Our goal is to explore this house and unpack its many boxes, but facing the writing head-on can feel like trying to enter this house through an imposing and locked steel front door. It can feel like a duel, a confrontation, the next impossible battle at hand.

Coming at the writing sideways allows me to gently ease my way in, to relax and breathe and get comfortable instead of seizing up, bracing for the attack. It is far too hard to write this chapter on coming at writing sideways—it's too big of a job for me! But if I were going to write about writing sideways I would say to myself: just put something down that you yourself would want to read, not what you imagine the big, intimidating angry literary critics would want you to write. Pretend this is yours, act as if. "Write what you would write if you were writing it," I say to my brain, to trick it. Fool even yourself until—surprise!—you have written a chapter through the trap door, climbing up the ivy and through the window instead of ringing the doorbell and waiting for someone else's permission to come in. Sneak through the cracks in the floor.

I've had articles to write that scared the shit out of me, so I wrote them sideways and they were nearly complete in the first draft. A student was asked to write her grandmother's eulogy, and in the midst of her grief, it was too big a task. I can't do this, she said. It's too big and too important. But if I were going to do this, this is what I would do. And she wrote the perfect, beautiful eulogy for her grandmother. Coming at it sideways, she told me, was just right.

Under Construction

We don't all live in a single-family house with a picket fence. We might live in a yurt or a tent or an igloo or a skyscraper. We might live in our car or on a friend's couch or in foster care or an ice palace. We don't all have to write five paragraph essays with topic sentences or a screenplay in three acts. Of course, like clichés, many of the tropes of writing have stuck around because they work, but that doesn't mean something else you want to write won't. I love reading six word memoirs, selections of flash non-fiction, micro-fiction, books written about colors in a numbered list.

Sometimes we are lucky to be gifted with an innate sense of structure, but sometimes we have to create the foundation and build the walls and erect the ceilings before we even know what kind of building we have under construction. Sometimes we have to put our intricate blueprints aside and ask the writing itself how it wants to be written. This might sound hokey, but try it. We might think we've set out to build a castle with a moat when the material we actually have to work with would better build a tree house. Does the voice of the mad scribble in your notebook want to continue on its own as a monologue? Does the journal entry about your mother lend itself to a blog post about your own journey as a mother?

Maybe as you describe your dozen-plus adopted siblings, each one will agree to occupy their own chapter. Maybe you need to create some line breaks to allow your smashed together prose space to move as a poem.

Often the things I plan to write become something else. I've created disparate pieces of writing I finally realized belonged together. I have drafts underway I still don't know what to do with. I'm hoping they will tell me someday. But if they are simply stepping stones between the houses I've built that are actually ready for inhabitants, that's OK too. Our writing will grow and take on a structure of its own, if we let it.

Running Through the Museum

You might need to write every day. You might need to write once a year on New Year's Eve or on your birthday or the anniversary of your cat's death. You might need to write at five a.m. with coffee and candles or at midnight under the moon in a circle of howling wolves. You might need to write in a class full of strangers or in a writing group or by yourself in a hole in the ground. You might need to process the hell you've survived for several years before you write your first publishable story. You might need to write 10 million angst-ridden poems before you write your literary novel. You might need to write all summer and hibernate all winter.

There is no formula for when and how much and how often you should write. Find your own rhythm. Find your own pace. The only thing that definitely does *not* work is berating yourself for the rhythm or pace that you have. Shame, guilt and whips have never worked productively for me long-term. If you write for 10 minutes a week, fine. If you only write when you are on vacation or in a class, fine.

A writing mentor once told me that reading my writing was like running through a museum. "I know the paintings are beautiful," she said, "but you never let me stop to look at them." She was right, but I needed to write that way for a very long time, and sometimes I still do. When I first started a regular writing practice, everything in my life felt so rushed and out of control and urgent that if I didn't get it all down in that moment, I felt I never would. Urgently was the only way I could write. In the years since I have slowed down. I have started to look more deeply into the paintings and moments and stories of my life. But at first I had to run as fast as I could to get through them, to know I wouldn't die in the heat of their fire.

I've had to find my own pace, my own rhythm, my own stride. I couldn't rush that process any more than I could write the book someone else wanted me to write.

Find your own pace, and trust it.

Polyester Patchwork Quilt

When I was living in Arkansas I bought a polyester patchwork quilt at a flea market on the side of the road. It was bright, cheerful and bawdy. None of the fluorescent orange, paisley or plaid panels matched but somehow, to me, it made perfect sense and brought me comfort during many odd nights on the road. Even though it shouldn't have, somehow, the whole thing worked together. And this is also how I see my writing process.

I have never been able to operate in sequence or follow the order of repetitive tasks. I don't advocate forced chronology if that's not how it comes to you in the moment. When I sit down to write, I rarely, if ever, start at the beginning of what I want to say. One of the phrases repeated most often in my long term writing group was, "Cut out the first half. Your story starts in the middle."

We are not going to sit down and start writing page one of our memoirs or novels and continue straight through to the epilogue. We are going to create one weird polyester patch that belongs somewhere in the middle. And then we are going to write a floral square that will get sewn into the bottom left. At first our sequence might not have any rhyme or reason. But if we keep creating our squares, as disparate as they may seem, they will eventually begin to fit together in a pattern that feels surprisingly complete.

Snakes on Medusa's Head

I was called a creative speller in elementary school. I'd rather claim "creative license" than correct some mistakes. I love mimicking the action of tossing "spelling, punctuation and grammar" out the window with my younger students when we first start a class. "I believe in editing too," I'm sure to tell them. "I was an editor. But in the first drafts we don't edit. We let our imaginations run wild."

And that's solid advice. The only problem is that if we only write first drafts and avoid editing completely, we avoid finishing. And finishing feels good. Not finishing your work is like baking a cake you never get to eat.

A friend of mine who is a lawyer and a writer said that editing is like throwing up and then trying to make a meal out of the chunks. Unfortunately, I have to agree. I have big unwieldy manuscripts stashed away in drawers with plots more tangled than the snakes on Medusa's head.

While I am often too loose with edits, I can also be too rigid. It helps if I limit the amount of time I allow myself to edit a piece or I will fidget with it forever, endlessly moving words like rats around a maze. A few years ago when I set the goal of publishing one piece a week on my blog, I gave myself a time limit. I had one hour to select the piece, type it and polish it up. These were short pieces but I could have spent weeks on each one. The one-hour time limit worked. An online literary journal asked to republish the very first piece I edited in this way. That never happened again but I took it as a good sign.

The most tried and true advice for editing I can use regularly is to create distance. Give yourself at least a couple of days or weeks away from your work to get a fresh perspective. Sleep on it. Then, when you are ready, come back, set the timer and wrestle gently with the snakes.

Writing a Bridge

Sometimes we need to write about writing. Sometimes we need to list all the reasons we love to write, or why we hate to write or what we want to write about.

I write because I want to find out what I think, how I feel, why I believe and who I am underneath the makeup and the clothing and the skin. I write because writing is the best revenge and the best way to avoid goodbye. I write because it's a vehicle for feelings that didn't want to take the train. I write because it's a more colorful version of black and white. I write because it's the grown up version of passing notes. I write because I'm tone deaf and I can't sing but I want to be heard. I write because I've found that even the littlest, weirdest, most obscure thought in my head, once written down, is somehow universal. I write because I am my own scientific laboratory, testing ground, petri dish, experiment, lab rat, not only for how I feel but for how others feel, too. I write because I am the universal I, the big and the little me, the hole in the donut and the whole donut, perfect in my imperfection, unique just like everyone else. I write to fit in and I write to stand out. I write because like Lord Byron says, if I don't write to empty my mind, I go mad. I write to feel better and to feel anything at all, good, bad, beautiful, horrible and so on, forever.

Sometimes we have to process the process. Sometimes we can't get to the fertile island of our story without building a bridge out of words to walk across. I think of bridge pieces as tune-ups for our vehicles, sharpening our tools, refining the paint in our palettes. Bridge pieces give us a chance to refocus and redirect when we get off course or don't know where the hell we're going.

Most of my writing plans, brainstorms and ideas emerge in bridge pieces. I think of this process as casting a wide net out into the sea and then sifting through what I've dragged to shore. This is not wasted writing; this is not wasted time. It is connective tissue, the way we get from here to there.

Reasons to Quit

It's all been done before. It's too hard. No one wants to hear what I think. What do I know? I don't want to burden anyone with my problems. I need to get a job. I need to make some money. No one will take me seriously. Writers are isolated shut-ins and I'm an extrovert. Writers have to interact with other people, and I'm an introvert. I need to get my addiction/divorce/foreclosure/wedding/degree/ 100th birthday party over with and taken care of first. There's something really interesting to watch on TV. I'd rather be reading. I'd rather be eating. I'd rather shoot myself in the face. My pen ran out of ink.

We can all come up with a thousand excuses not to write but none of them stand up to the pure and sacred satisfaction that comes from writing anyway, despite all the reasons not to do it. To avoid writing I have taken up basket-weaving, scrapbooking, stained glass making, traveling, bad relationships, moving, over-eating, drinking, drugs, toxic people, Facebook and cable TV.

But, because writing is core, primal, elemental and because I don't need permission or money or degrees or stability or a larger home to do it, I have returned to writing again and again. And every time it feeds me, nourishes me, gives me what I was really looking for in all of my other escapes and distractions. I do have to step away from time to time, but only as an intentional part of my practice, not to avoid it.

What are your reasons to quit? Do any of them hold water?

Underwhelming Goals

I urge writers to set underwhelming goals. We have enough pressure, stress and fear without piling on more. When we set sky high goals and fail to achieve them, we beat ourselves up mercilessly. When we lower the bar and set goals we can achieve blindfolded with our hands tied behind our backs, we feel proud and accomplished. We may even keep going!

I have tried both ways. And for me, only one way works with my sanity intact. While I have thrived under the pressure of stress and have been motivated by insults and criticisms, the work itself has suffered. It is contrived, forced, angry and written to please people I don't even like. I sought a militant discipline I had no idea how to achieve. I thought, that's what you had to do to be a writer.

Then my mother gave me a refrigerator magnet that says: "Discipline is remembering what you want." And I liked that. It helped me breathe. I want a happy life full of inspired writing, not the regimented life of a Marine. When I ease up, speak sweetly to myself and stop feeling like the world will end and I will die if I don't get everything done yesterday, true writing begins to emerge.

For the first two years of my son's life I met

with a weekly writing group every Tuesday night. A new mother, struggling to juggle the many demands of life, I set the underwhelming goal of writing one page a week. And I did! It felt tremendous. I don't give my classes homework because sometimes just showing up for writing class is a huge feat in and of itself. But at the end of class I do offer everyone a chance to set an intention, if they'd like. When I hear "chapter" or "finish" I see a red flag and urge writers to rein it in. Perhaps try to write for 10 minutes one time this week, I suggest. And then sometimes that 10 minutes feels so good, so possible, it becomes 20. But that's not our goal. Our goal is to begin.

IV. MY STORY

Tell the Truth

I was seven when I told my mother I wanted to grow up to be a famous reader. I devoured many books every week and was often forced to go outside to play so I could get hit in the head with a dodge ball like everyone else. My eighth grade story won the class contest and at that point my desire to be a famous reader merged with the idea that I could maybe be a writer, too.

I was on the staff of the literary magazine in high school and went to a creative writing camp for young writers at the University of Virginia Young Writer's Workshop, where for a few weeks of summer we lived in the dorms, experimented with form and style and voice and point of view, fell in love with each other, were treated as real writers and not just kids with a hobby. I cried for weeks when I got back home.

When I was 17, my mother encouraged me to write to Madeleine L'Engle, my idol, and ask permission to attend a writing workshop she was teaching at the Omega Institute in upstate New York even though the minimum age requirement was 18. She said yes and I took my first memoir workshop from my living idol, the writer who had drawn me into the world of the imagination, fantasy and worlds beyond what we could see. But her workshop, "Writing the

Truth," started much closer to home, with the personal narrative. I wrote my first true story then about my dad's divorce from my first stepmother and how they both ended up in rehab the summer I turned 10.

Madeleine, already in her 70's, was a mystical force who had published nearly a hundred books and gave me permission to write about my own small, personal world as a 17-year-old remembering what it was like to be 10. It was a tremendous gift and though I wrote fiction for years, learning to explore and tell the truth was a North Star that would always lead me home.

Humble Pie

When I was 18 and a freshman at Sarah Lawrence, a very small and very liberal arts college in New York, I submitted 10 one-page pieces of flash fiction to the school-wide fiction contest. Those stories won me first place, $200 and an award presented by Grace Paley, who had once been a prominent teacher at my school. Only, I had misunderstood the contest and thought I was going to win $2,000. Also, I didn't yet really know who Grace Paley was. I would only fall in love with her writing later, awed by our meeting years after the fact. While I was pleased I had won the contest, I was crushed that I hadn't won enough money to buy a plane ticket to the Dominican Republic to visit one of my best friends living there.

When I showed these stories to a boy in my dorm, he looked up at me with his green eyes and golden skin and tousled blonde hair and said in his French accent, "you really need to travel." And at that point, even though my writing was the heart and grit and salt of me, I set out to prove him wrong, accept his challenge, and annihilate the words that proved I was a dirty, poor girl from Virginia and always would be while he drank fine wine in his chateau and read the real writers—the writers who had traveled. Unintentionally, he sent me on a heartsick quest to prove I could find in the world that which he didn't find in my writing—glamor, adventure, worldliness, polish, everything as far outside of myself as I could get. As I rode the tram in Amsterdam, visited castles in Tuscany, crossed golden bridges in Prague, listened to the choirs of Vienna and visited the baths of Budapest I thought, "look at me now, see how I've changed." But he could not and I could not because everything I really had to say was waiting to be written inside of me, not in another country or foreign lands.

Meanwhile, a boy in my freshman fiction workshop invited me to go see Alice Walker talk about female genital mutilation in New York City and we kissed on the subway car back to campus, but I didn't go out with him again after that. He was simply too kind, too nice, too encouraging, too sincere. That nice, sincere boy went on to become the Senior Fiction Editor at Viking Penguin, a fact I discovered flipping through the back pages of our quarterly alumni journal. Swallowing down horror at the memory of my blind stupidity, I called to interview him about the state of the publishing world for an article I was writing and he was very generous with his knowledge and time, and for that I am grateful.

Live Your Life

As a 19 year-old camp counselor at the young writer's workshop I had gone to as a high school student, I requested a day off to attend a backyard barbecue hosted by The White Pygmy Queen in honor of her good friend, Tom Robbins. My mother had been commissioned to make buttons for the party and said she would do so on the condition that they invite her and her daughter. We arrived with potato salad and lawn chairs.

Unbeknownst to me, my mother had a sheaf of my stories squirreled away in her purse which she gave to my literary idol at the end of the party. He told her he'd read them on the plane. If he did, I can only imagine how much they read like Tom Robbins Fan Fiction. His exuberant, outrageous language set my teenage heart on fire and I mimicked his style with a vengeance. Several times during the barbeque I was mistaken for his newest wife, also very young and also in a dress of floral polyester.

When I finally got my big one-on-one with The Man he told me that if I really wanted to be a writer I should drop out of my college writing program immediately and do something useful like travel the world or go to nursing school. I argued this point with him vehemently, disinclined to drop the writing program that had offered me such generous financial aid and scholarship assistance or the young writer's workshop that had treated me like a writer and changed my life forever. But I did find in the years that I traveled after graduation—to become a cabin girl on a dude ranch in Colorado, a hotel maid on a mountain in Arkansas and a stewardess on a cruise ship in Alaska—that by living my life I gathered some of the most valuable material I could hope for in this lifetime. I believe that Tom Robbins was right, but that I was right too. It's a both/and situation. Studying writing and living your life are not mutually exclusive.

Publication

When I was pregnant with my son I took a fiction class at the Virginia Museum. I had recently been through a death in the family, a series of surgeries, several miscarriages and hadn't written in any regular way since I'd graduated from college in New York. I felt very disconnected from the world of writing, from myself as a writer, in fact from the dream of ever writing anything down again. I was working as an administrative assistant at an all-boys middle school and I was pregnant and exhausted, but the class at the museum energized me and I looked forward to Tuesday nights all week long.

In that class I met a guy who worked at both Home Depot and *Style*, the local alternative weekly in Richmond. He might as well have told me he was a senior editor at the *New Yorker*. Writing regularly, much less professionally, seemed like such a beautiful but impossible dream.

"How is it that you write for *Style*?" I asked him one night after class on our way out to the parking lot. "How is it that you don't?" he asked back. I spent the entire week chewing it over and had my answer prepared by the following Tuesday night. "I have a million good excuses why I haven't written in the past," I told him. "But I don't have any for the future. What do I do?" In the parking lot of the Virginia Museum I was walked through the steps of finding my material, pitching an idea and writing an article.

I got started that week, focusing on a banned book reading festival at a local bookstore. My friend introduced me to his editor and I pitched my story. She accepted and published it—after re-writing almost every single word. Still, I was thrilled and had the article laminated at Kinko's. I pitched another story the very next week. "I *guess* I'll give you another chance," she said, and then, very generously, over the phone walked me through the most egregious of my errors. I studied them like the Bible, wrote my second article and she published it without changing a word.

Writers, Queens and Gods

I was offered the job of Book Editor at *Style* five months later, the week my son was born. I thought it was the most glamorous job in the world even though I couldn't cover a whole utility bill with my paycheck. I didn't get the job because of my credentials but because I was eager, enthusiastic, punctual and available when the other book editor quit. I took on the job like a calling to the clergy, with all of my heart.

Those seven years were like hands-on grad school for me, providing an opportunity to interview a great number of incredible writers, well known or up-and-coming. Each interview was an education in genre, style, dialogue, perseverance, dedication, luck and inspiration.

Jonathan Safran Foer and I chatted by phone, but he only had the walk of a few city blocks in his schedule so I had to stretch his words like oil in the temple. Tom Wolfe graciously answered a few of my questions after the Library of Virginia's Literary Awards ceremony—but I never turned on my tape recorder, failed to write a single word down and had to ad-lib my impressions in what became a pretty funny essay about new journalism, those writers who succeed and those who fail at their craft. Lee Smith was the soul of generosity, kindness and Southern Hospitality. I hung on her every word hoping to inhale some of her gorgeous literary spirit through osmosis.

I listened to Toni Morrison in a stadium of thousands and we worshipped like we were all in mega church with the one true prophet of God. I trekked into the city to hear the profound wisdom of Maya Angelou who was like an angel in skin using her words as prayer to bless us all. Jeannette Walls invited me into her beautiful farmhouse in the mountains of western Virginia, introduced me to her iconic mother, entertained and awed me for hours with her beautiful spirit and confided in me that you can say absolutely anything you want about anyone you write about as long as you describe them as being very physically attractive.

I was blown away by *The 99th Monkey: A Spiritual Journalist's Misadventures with Gurus, Messiahs, Sex, Psychedelics, and Other Consciousness-Raising Experiments*, and was thrilled to discover that the author, Eliezer Sobel, lived in town and before long, welcomed him into my family as a friend. Professor Shawna Kenney, author of the underground cult classic *I Was a Teenage Dominatrix*, and David Henry Sterry, author of *Chicken: Self Portrait of a Young Man for Rent*, took me into the world of sex workers, transformation, transparency and empowerment. During a phone interview, Azar Nafisi, the author of *Reading Lolita in Tehran* told me that "reading is the only place we can allow ourselves to be promiscuous." Journalist, memoirist, teacher and author of *The Journal Keeper*, Phyllis Theroux took me under her wing and into her home, dazzling me with the power of the intimate conversation between a writer and her journal.

I interviewed numerous other local, national and international authors during my time as a book reviewer. They were all kisses from the great beyond, lamp posts lighting up the dark journey of finding my own way and voice as a writer.

Literary Snobs

I adored *Ruby Fruit Jungle*, a feminist literary masterpiece about the coming of age of a young lesbian, and asked Rita Mae Brown during our interview why she had turned from literary fiction to her cat and fox/hound mystery series. "Literary snobs are my greatest pet peeve," she roared into the phone. "They need their crutch," she told me. "Don't take it away from them; it's cruel." She was kind to me, though I still couldn't understand the allure of writing a book that didn't appeal to the highest literary sensibilities, that *anyone* might want to read.

Now that I have edged myself out of the world of literary elitism her words echo and resonate. I love the stories of the landscaper and waitress and parking lot owner, the stay-at-home mom, the yoga teacher, the therapist and priest. It is honesty, vulnerability and bravery that I get the most from in my classes, not pedigrees or publishing credits.

Service & Work

While I was the book editor at *Style*, I was asked to join the board of James River Writers, a nonprofit for readers and writers in the central Virginia region, and thus continued my education in the world of reading, writing and publication. For two years I produced the monthly panel "The Writing Show," and served for one year as the vice chair of the annual conference. Volunteering my time in the service of writing gave me back far more than I was able to give. I was immersed in a community of writers of every background, genre and level of experience, widening my view of who you had to be to write, to publish, to find a sense of belonging in the writing world. Lucky for me and many others, Richmond has a rich, diverse and vibrant writing scene. I have been able to ask for advice, feedback and support from such talented local authors, poets and writers as Gigi Amateau, Julie Geen, Bird Cox, Stephenie Brown, Hope Whitby, Slash Coleman, Darren Morris, Anne Thomas Soffee, Ellen Brown, Virginia Pye, Anne Westrick, Patty Smith, Meg Medina, Susann Cokal, Katharine Herndon and *many others* right here in my own home town.

When I was laid off from my desk job with benefits and decided to start Richmond Young Writers and creative nonfiction classes for adults, I had a rich community from which to draw support and connection. Initially, choosing to teach small groups in the backs of bookstores rather than getting a full time job with benefits forced me to question my own sanity, stability and ability to keep a bank account in the black. But that choice has paid off handsomely in richness of spirit and quality of life.

After years of teaching in coffee shops and bookstores, my classes now have their own dedicated space in the heart of the city attached to the eclectic and vibrant independent new and used bookstore, Chop Suey Books. Richmond Young Writers has a brilliant and dedicated staff of teachers and interns who serve hundreds of wildly creative kids in special programs throughout the year, offering scholarships to those in need. My adult classes, workshops and retreats are filled with people of a vast range of occupations, backgrounds and levels of experience who continuously inspire and awe me with their stories, their originality, their honesty, their beauty.

I often thank my students for showing up to class so that I can have the space and structure to write and they laugh at me, but it's true. Hearing my own fears, neurosis, misconceptions, false beliefs and insecurities around writing echoed in the room has given me a new lens with which to view my own process. They say you teach what you need to learn and in my case that has certainly been true.

Writing Teacher

Some days I am overwhelmed by the preciousness, the sanctity of what I do. I feel like a priest or a bartender, a hairdresser, taking everyday confessions, narratives, snapshots and deep inner revelations, while also getting to shape my own. I want the whole world to see and hear experience the wonder of what I do.

Life in 10 Minutes is a start, a portal for the stories to pour through. But these stories have back stories and the way they are filtered through me makes me yearn to synthesize them all into a great orchestra, a master work to show and sing—but that's another Everest and these stories are the hills and potholes we climb over and stumble into every day, that I wrap myself in like the clothes I put on in the morning.

The archivist whose four great aunts were hermaphrodites growing up in the 1930s, or the writer who moved here after her husband had a sex change and both of their new boyfriends moved in and everything blew up, the heroic single mothers and single dads paving their way through hurricanes with the shovel of grace, the parents whose children are gone or grieving or lost or addicted, the mother whose mother was murdered, the priest who feels like his is the most feral family on the block, the breakups and the reunions, the engagements, the job changes and house moves, the battles with bureaucracy and broken systems, what to eat, whom to love, God, Jesus, Buddha, death, birth, sex, the resurrection of dead dreams.

It is the music under the waves of my every day. I can't fix it or eat it or change it or wear it so I put it on the page and name it. Bearing witness is an honor, and my amazement is my prayer. My own broken, healing, body and heart and marriage and life carried along on the backbone and stories and revelations of yours.

Thank you for sharing your stories with me.

V. MY WRITING

When I Was Born

When I was born my father saw a comet shoot through the universe and when it hit the earth he heard my first cry.

When I was one our house was full of cats and art and smoke.

When I was two I put the peanut in the place I saw my mother put the tampon.

When I was two I knew the difference between a joint and a cigarette.

When I was two I ate a cigarette.

When I was two my dad left and my grandmother died and my mother quit drinking and smoking.

When I was three I walked around the house saying, "Where's Daddy?" When I was three I said my first poem: "Lightbug, moon, home."

When I was four I told my mother my angels were with me. When I was four I dreamt there were lions in our front yard.

When I was four I took all my pictures off the walls because my mother was in the hospital and I didn't think she was coming back.

When I was five the kindergarten teacher took the boys into the closet and pinched their dark brown ears until they turned bright red.

When I was five another teacher, a storyteller, the one who saved my soul in elementary school, named me Laughing Rainbow.

When I was six a classmate accused me of starting slavery. When I was six I learned to be really, really nice. When I was six I won the Good Citizenship Award at my school.

When I was seven I told my mother I wanted to grow up to be a famous reader. When I was seven I asked my dad to marry me.

When I was eight I rubbed scraped knees with a friend and we became blood sisters.

When I was nine we lined our Barbies up along the bed as prostitutes and Ken was the pimp.

When I was ten I wanted to be a grownup and my mother said, "Don't wish your life away."

When I was eleven I played softball and got a perm and wore blue eye shadow.

When I was twelve I wore a giant styrofoam dragon costume I'd made at summer camp to my first boy-girl party where all of the other girls were catwomen and cheerleaders.

When I was thirteen I told my mother I was ready to move out and get my own apartment.

When I was thirteen I told my mother I couldn't learn from her mistakes, I would have to learn from my own.

When I was thirteen I decided that my goal in life was to experience everything.

Where I'm From

I am from the little lady with the big baby. The little lady who carved us naked out of clay, me sprawled fat and naked and barely born across her belly, fired hard and brown in the oven.

I am from the little boy with the pet crow and a foot so long they said he looked like an "L" with hands, I've discovered, mine will never actually grow into.

I'm from Jewish anarchists and Methodist peacekeepers, garden gnomes and Denmark, Boris and Margaret, Whilhelmina and Ray, the Pale—that stretch of land between Poland and Russia.

I'm from the Shenandoah Valley and MCV, a little house with a big backyard in a ghetto of the west end in a corner of the world called Tuckahoe, a name I've heard means "Little Potato."

I am from short and tall, late and early, passive aggressive and just aggressive, tongues that whip and kiss and bite, pray and sing and eat. I am from a grated oil floor furnace and metal ducts snaking forced heat through holes in the wall, couches found in alleys, lampshades made by hand, food stamps, thrift stores, love first rate, big, shiny, bright.

I am from pastel and oil, acrylic and watercolor, pencil and ink, wood and ruler, hammer and nail, chisel, chainsaw, miter, drill, screw.

I am from Mr. Rogers and Bob Marley, Uncle Wiggly and The Rainbow Goblins, The Monkey King and Thumbelina.

I am from marriage and divorce, love and its opposites, the familiar clang of the world at its beginning, splitting apart and then reformed, broken and whole, the friction and velvet of two people working out their distances across town, across a river, across a little girl.

I am from blooming fig trees and hacked down dogwoods, watermelon rinds, black licorice sticks, mugs of Folgers shot through with honey and hot milk.

I am from a house full of art and cats and paint and dishes piled high in the sink, addiction treated and untreated, words in sentences, books and stories, broken becoming whole again and again and again.

Love Was

Love was Kenneth, the only boy in kindergarten who didn't chase or pinch me on the playground.

Love was the red heart post earrings left on my front porch by the boy I got in trouble for hitting.

Love was playing Cinderella in the back of the pinto station wagon while my mom was in yoga with a little boy for whom being the prince meant showing me his butt.

Love was all of my mother's boyfriends and all of my father's girlfriends and wondering who I was going to grow up to be.

Love was the wrangler I was engaged to who couldn't spell my name, and his dad who called me Cowgirl.

Love was slow-dancing to Desperado around the campfire and not falling in.

Love was the cutouts of male underwear models my new boyfriend hung in his room because they reminded him of him.

Love was being offered the presidential suite flying down the highway, convertible top down, his wedding ring on.

Love was holding his gun in the backseat of the car.

Love was taking my hair down out of the barrette as he called me his greatest enemy.

Love was down on my knees in the broken glass of the alley.

Love was locking everyone else out and locking ourselves in.

Love was naming a star from the International Star Registry after me and giving me the framed certificate. Even if it's fake. I don't care if it's fake.

Love was knowing who I was going to marry while losing at Trivial Pursuit on our very first date, right after dinner.

Love was trying and trying and trying and trying 1,000 times again.

Love was discovering through a series of days unfolding and birth and blood and my heart broken open that boys, too, are human.

16 Ways to Say I Do

1. When I go pee, I drop my veil in the toilet.

2. Before everyone arrives, my dad and I walk up and down the country road, tying butterfly balloons to posts and picking up beer bottles and Doritos bags.

3. I decide to take his last name after the rehearsal dinner. Changing my name feels bigger and stranger than getting married.

4. I write my vows before anyone else wakes up, before the sun rises in morning.

5. One of my bridesmaids has to attend a birth that morning but she makes it back in time to hold her bouquet that afternoon.

6. The man who catches the boutonniere is in a wheelchair then and is dead now.

7. Almost everybody who attends Stan's bachelor party is dead now too: AIDS, cancer, suicide.

8.	I'm afraid I'll fall in the lake in my wedding dress but my new husband is able to steady the canoe.

9.	Our minister is actually a priestess who'd performed a past life Rohun ceremony on me to clear away all of the energetic blockages keeping me from happy relationships the week before Stan asked me on our first date and I give a session with her to all of my bridesmaids.

10.	My friend who lives in a yurt sings Amazing Grace.

11.	It rained so much the night before the tent posts sink deep into the ground but our wedding day is bright and sunny.

12.	At the last minute I decide to go barefoot and all my bridesmaids do too.

13.	I pick splinters of bird-seed and rice out of the soles of my feet in our hotel room.

14.	We are the eighth married couple the chauffeur at the Jefferson escorts that day.

15.	I knew I was meant to marry Stan on

our first date and I don't for a moment doubt it now.

16.   Still, I cry uncontrollably as my dad walks me down the aisle.

I Remember You

I remember the day you were born by emergency C-section, how blood flew everywhere, even the doctor's faces. The cord was wrapped so many times around your neck they had to spin you around like a top to unravel you, and then you mewed like a kitten and latched on to your father's nose as he held you on the way to bring you to me. I remember how you blamed yourself that the other babies didn't make it and turned everything you could —even twigs or scraps of food—into baby brothers. I remember in the bathtub when you told me that you'd thought you were going to be born a girl and I told you I was just so glad you were born at all. I remember when you found the ultrasounds from the others in the attic and you put them on the fridge under magnets next to your own drawings and school photos. I remember the letter I wrote you in my journal the day you accused me of being more of a person than a parent, explaining how I could never explain how much I love you, how very wanted you are. I remember when you asked to have your room decluttered for Christmas, how for your birthday you asked for experiences rather than things. I remember when you named me "Rainbow," your father "Hungry" and yourself "Diaper." I can't remember how many times I've swelled with pride at your beauty, your intelligence, humor and athletic prowess. I remember wanting to claim all of you but wondering how the hell you came from me.

Pest Control

At one point in our marriage we let our home become overrun by cockroaches. It was like one of the plagues out of the Old Testament—a punishment we would simply have to endure, a pestilence we were powerless to control, anymore than we could have controlled locusts or boils or the death of first-borns. I feel like I'm telling you I let my toddler eat dog food—which I did but only because he loved it so much and our mailman assured me that all of his children had eaten dog food too and turned out just fine.

It started slow. One little cockroach scurrying from Point A to Point B across the kitchen counter. But it escalated quickly and the invaders began to conquer other territories of the house. The dining room. The living room. Our bedroom. We bought Raid and little cockroach motels but all of our attempts to help ourselves were fruitless, spitting into the wind. And for a long time—weeks? months?—instead of asking for help, instead of calling one of the dozens of pest control enterprises in town, we did nothing.

And I think this is because, to some degree or another, we were both in complete despair. Our marriage consisted of bitter fights and angry silences. Neither of us worked enough to cover all of our bills and we each expected the other to do it, but neither of us would. I sought relief in an online affair, and my husband in hours of shooting zombies in video games, both of us living out fantasy lives instead of rebuilding the ones we actually had. Projects went unstarted or unfinished. Every night we ate ramen noodles or rice and beans or whatever else required minimal effort. We felt stuck and angry, like the state of our house and marriage was happening to us, not because of us. Eventually everything blew up, and from that point on began to improve. We called pest control, and a therapist. The cockroaches and despair are gone and I miss neither one.

Question in Class: "How Did You Stop Hating Yourself?"

How have I stopped hating myself? I'm still working on it, but it has become a point of study for me, a focused inquiry. I haven't tried to write about it directly yet, so this is definitely tumbling head over heels down the mountain in the middle of the avalanche. I think first I had to realize that the self-criticisms, insults and smack-talk actually were a form of self-hatred, not helpful reminders I needed to get through the day. To start to see "you goddamned stupid idiot, I can't believe you forgot trash day again, only assholes forget trash day" as actual abuse and not a handy way of helping myself remember trash day next week was a start.

Just like dogs thrive on positive reinforcement, so do children, so do we. If I behaved better, achieved more and was more efficient and productive as a result of berating myself, I would still do it. But it doesn't work. I cower under my own self-abuse. I freeze, I stop, I forget again. And it's usually the smallest, dumbest things that trigger a tirade of damning criticisms. The big things, of course—you're a fake, a whore, so ghetto, an underachiever, never lived up to potential, wannabe, etc. I'm not sure anyone else even ever said these things to me—they didn't have to. I said them enough myself. It's a practice to stop cursing myself out, to cut off the verbal abuse and transform my self-talk, the monologue in my head into gentle, soft, loving words, the same words I would give to anyone else. I don't want to be a hypocrite, loving and accepting you but hating and beating up me. I don't want to waste any more precious time.

The other day I told a friend I really need to get my eating under control, currently the biggest element of chaos in an otherwise beautiful life. Like today I accidentally ate two hot dogs as a snack instead of a carrot, and I feel such hot shame for not being a vegan juicer, for treating my body more like a carnival than a temple, and she said, "Stop. We love you just the way you are," and that's when the tears came and a new wave of healing washed over me because how crazy is that? To be loved just the way I am? Can I love myself, hungry for everything, starving for all of life, more than my share? I think it's a good place to start.

What, if I don't find a way
to say it, will kill me?

The unsaid? I think my mother's just about said it all. At a reading we did together in the city when I was 17, her piece began: "All I did was open my legs twice and this is what I got?" There have been several conversations I wish required more imagination. But now it's my turn. I have a voice, a story, a pen and a website and I'm navigating the tricky terrain—vast, cavernous—through what can be said in a public forum and what's between me and Jesus (not that me and Jesus spend that much time talking but I did hear he has a thing for Jewish girls). Everyone in my life gives me stories but can they stomach the same stories read back to them? Can I?

When I asked my husband how he felt about appearing regularly in a public forum he said, "I think I gave you that permission in my wedding vows." But did he really? Can he begin to predict what I might feel more comfortable writing than saying? How much is too much? If I overuse the F-word and the G-D word and write about my heathen life as it really is, can I ever face my sweet and dearly beloved mother-in-law again? I have always heard and truly believe from the writers I love that the most important thing to do first is the writing itself. Everything that follows is under the jurisdiction of the second draft, the editor, the logic brain. But what if the logic brain is scared to death? What if the logic brain is broken? What if all I've got is what just comes out? How much is too much, and what, if I don't find a way to say it, will kill me?

Passing Notes to Friends and Strangers

I'm writing today to honor my view out the window of the emerald monster green dumpster, the coiled garden hose ready to strike, the shovel stabbed at an angle into the frozen earth.

I'm writing even though I exhausted the possibility of becoming a teenage prodigy 100 or 30 years ago.

I write to resist the compulsion to erase, scratch through, burn or bury every word.

I write as the alchemy with which I turn my most tangled snarls into specimens of interest to examine from more than just the one angle.

I write as a grown-up version of passing notes to friends and strangers.

I write with the vision of a queen transformed into a bar wench dancing on the table, her skirt wrapped around her head.

I write because the cost of not writing is more than I can afford to pay.

I write because it's free.

I write as mental hygiene.

I write because the page is the vacation home for my brain.

I write because I have an addictive personality and it's better than getting drunk or high or STDs.

I write because it pairs well with coffee.

I write because I can't kiss the feet of each remarkable moment but I can write them down and share them with you.

Halfway House for Writers

I have been overwhelmed and grateful and surprised but also surprisingly neurotic about the intro/birth/launch of my baby/project, Life in 10 Minutes. I have to keep reminding myself (with a little help from my super intelligent friends) that this is about the process, not the finished product, or approval or likes or comments or little exploding heart icons at the bottom of a post. The quality of submissions I've already received has been so amazingly high that I've had moments of deep shame about posting my own writing, which suddenly seems like a runny nosed kindergartner bursting into a room full of grad students holding their degrees. *Here I am!* I yell. *Look at me!* But there's paint and snot and mud and grammatical errors all over my face and I still don't know my ABCs.

I want to turn tail and run from the room but I can't because I just finished building the walls — with a lot of help from my outrageously talented friends. So, I say to myself what I say to my students every day. Stop comparing. You can't judge your own writing. You don't know what you've done or where you'll end up, only that you must keep going. And so I'm trying to stay still in the practice of not knowing. Of writing scared, but writing. I already know well the practice of editing a single sentence down past its bone. Of keeping quiet and being nice and holding the worst of it in. Of seeing what I lack and the sum total of my deficits. What I'm learning is to trust the voice that comes, in my writing and my life. What I'm learning is to put it out there true, as it is, in my writing and my life.

One man, an old friend, a lawyer, called my class a Halfway House for Writers. And it rang true. A Halfway House in which we're all neurotic and damaged and halfway insane but getting better, healing, recovering, together.

Competitive Depression

Right now, after a deep and miserable 24 hour funk, I'm back. I realized this morning that not only was I depressed, I was actually in a competitive depression with my husband. If he's low I have to be lower. I have to one-up him, I have to be more depressed. He can't get *all* the glory. Of all the things I've realized about myself, this may be one of the worst. Like last week when a friend and I realized we are competitive eaters. He's not getting more pizza than me—oh no, he *isn't!* Two areas in which one has absolutely no business trying to compete: overeating and misery.

Yay, I'm a winner!

Well, it's good to recognize, accept and hopefully let go. To make up for it this morning I did all the things I could think of to feel better (without drinking Wild Turkey, shooting up or looking for a cowboy). A long slow run, morning pages, my spinach/spirulina/dirt/banana smoothie, 290 vitamins, huffing an essential oil blend, taking an actual shower, and now I find myself trying to be competitively happy and well-adjusted. At least I have my priorities straight.

So many dear friends are having total breakdowns right now, or as they are also known, spiritual awakenings. I think sometimes spiritual awakenings happen at your lowest, bottomest, most exposed, humiliated and broken times. So I'm not only sad for my friends in crisis right now, I'm a little competitively jealous too. Dammit, their bottom looks worse than mine! They are going to have bigger and better spiritual awakenings! I should start training for the Spiritual Olympics. 40 Crisis Crunches before the Breakdown 10K followed by the Prayerful Sobbing Javelin Throw.

Sadly enough, I'll probably train as hard as I can to win.

Last Night of Writing Class

Right now I am trying to slow down a mind that has suddenly switched from "let's explore our inner self" to compulsively Type A, hyper-organized and insanely product oriented. Switching into summer work mode, I've tackled my task lists like a sumo wrestler. I feel like I've been trying to climb Mount Trashmore and organize a lifetime of accumulated trash, but with mindful awareness. Although to be fair I have leveled up from the dump pile. The stuff I'm tackling is far more sublime but just as endless, or so it seems today.

This morning I yelled at my husband after completing my morning affirmations, answered my phone twice during my 10 minute guided meditation and ran out of my hair appointment with sopping wet hair so I could make it to the last half of my 12 step meeting. I had a smoothie for breakfast and a glazed doughnut for lunch.

But at least I'm trying. Which is all so different from the haphazard, devil-may-care, fly by the seat of my pants days of yore when I jumped into everything unprepared, pre-research on gut instinct alone and then figured everything out— or not—while flying full speed ahead.

Right now I'm realizing this is my last

structured night of 10 minute writing for the next two months and I don't know what kind of life that means I will live. Will I write at all?

Will my life become more like a checklist than a paragraph?

Will I start to suffocate under the weight of accumulated untold stories?

Will I find myself at the notebook hungry out of pure need?

I created this structure because I finally accepted that I need it but maybe too I need the seasons and cycles of hibernation—time to go within and digest in silence without attention paid to every detail and twist. I don't know yet, only that when I return I will be ready like pre-wedding ready, pre-move ready, pre-deep sea diving, cave excavation ready to lay it all out on the page again.

While I Was Gone

Right now I am rusty like a lawn mower left outside, upside down in the rain. Right now I am wrapped in foil and saran—so many layers removed from the part of me beneath the skin next to the bone that allows me to be scrubbed clean by writing. Right now I'm on other planets, other galaxies, inside of other caves. I have taken a six-week hiatus from regular writing and it feels like six years, six lifetimes. I have written, yes. But not in the pressure cooker of a class where my hand can't stop, where I can't get up to see if anything new has magically appeared in the fridge, take a little dive into the ocean, run around the block just to distract myself from me. But, okay. Like a bear I need to hibernate every once in a while. though what I just imagined was a bear trying on tutus in a dressing room.

What I really want to say is I've been packing in the living. Teaching kids, turning 40, hitting the road with my family who feel like a real family now, not people I accidentally ended up living with, marrying and pushing out of my body. This motherhood gig is so wild. At first my contract seemed interminable and now I'm begging to extend the contract.

On the day before my husband's birthday, from the balcony of the beach house we got with friends, I watched a deer lope across the beach access road. I walked down to the beach as the sun rose, a fluorescent fiery ball of melon in a hurry to ascend the sky. Dolphins dove and jumped in tandem, their black fins synchronized like Olympic swimmers. Crabs formed a circle around me in the sand to spy on me with their enormous eyes googling around on the tops of their heads. On my way back to the house, a bunny big and fat and brown leapt across my path and I gasped at the ridiculousness of so many generous, unexpected gifts. That night we watched the sun plunk down through the clouds and into the sound. Everything was so much better than the summer, the trip, the life, I would have chosen.

Right now I'm ready to see what waits at the end of this pen even when I refuse for so long to uncap it.

VI. LIFE IN 10 MINUTES

10 Minutes at a Time

You do not have to be on a writer's retreat to have enough time to write. You don't even have to have a whole day or a whole hour. No matter your subject or genre, you can begin something new or continue something already begun, 10 minutes at a time.

Why 10 minutes?

Because what better way to eat the elephant, than 10 minutes at a time? Because even 10 minutes of bad writing is better than 10 minutes of not writing. Because it's hard to convince yourself you don't have 10 minutes. Because 10 minutes is a safe investment with surprising returns. Because 10 minutes can capture a snapshot of your life the way a thimbleful of water can capture the taste and temperature and consistency of the ocean. Because you can spend 10 minutes looking at photos of your old friend's uncle's priest's hairdresser's mother-in-law's trip to the beach, so you might as well spend 10 minutes writing.

Because you are guaranteed to find at least one thought or phrase or word packed with energy or mystery or surprise that encourages you to continue. Because committing to write for 10 minutes is less terrifying than committing to write a novel or a book or a screenplay or a thesis or a poem. Because 10 minutes is a pressure cooker with the heat set to high. Because you can do it now, without a degree or a PhD or your mother's approval or a license or a million-dollar vacation home or a week off of work or botox or perfect thighs or anyone's permission.

Because the longest journey begins with the first 10 minutes.

An Invitation

10 minutes is long enough to uproot your life, get caught in a storm, drink a cup of coffee, memorize a child's face, wash a sink full of dishes, recite wedding vows, fall in love with someone you shouldn't, eat a sandwich, remember a dream, call an old friend, sketch a figure model, read a chapter, listen to your favorite song, get on or off the train that will change the course of your life forever. 10 minutes is enough time to write something strange and beautiful and true without editing the strangeness and beauty and truth out of it.

We all have 10 minutes, many times a day, so it's hard to come up with convincing excuses—even to our secret innermost selves—why we don't. 10 minutes is everything we can't fit into a Facebook status; it's slice of life, short-shorts, a Polaroid picture, a poem, a prayer.

You have read some of mine—what stories from your life can you tell in 10 minutes? I invite you to share your raw, weird, surprising, heartbreaking, funny, unfinished, messy, beautiful stories with me at:

lifein10minutes.com

Write Now

Are you in the parking lot waiting for the grocery store to open? Are you on an airplane flying to Transylvania? Are you shivering in your tent in the base camp of Mount Everest? Are you on your couch in your curlers? Maybe you've set aside a day or an hour to write and the day is looming before you like the great Sahara. Great! This is a perfect time to get started.

Don't wait until you move to a more literary city or buy a new house or find the right veneer for your new writing desk. Don't wait until you've gotten it all together or figured it all out. Don't wait until you feel like a "real writer." Don't even wait until you know what it is you want to say. Don't worry yourself with whether or not you're good enough or if your writing career will ever "pan out." Don't wait until you're happier, sadder, saner, speak better English or have bought a thicker thesaurus. That day may not ever come. You have everything you need to get started now.

Sit down with some paper and a pen. Set a timer and write for 10 minutes without stopping. Keep the pen moving. Start with "Right Now I Am." When you are done, underline a word or phrase from what you've just written that still has energy in it, that asks for more to be said.

Use this word or phrase to jumpstart your next 10 minutes. Rinse and repeat. Keep it to yourself or share it widely. Revisit it tomorrow for revision or allow it to be a stepping stone to your next piece.

Either way, congratulations! You are writing. You have a found a room in the Halfway House for Writers. You are a *writer*. Have a cup of coffee or tea, settle in and make yourself at home. You are welcome to stay for as long as you like.

CPSIA information can be obtained at www.ICGtesting.com
Printed in the USA
BVOW06s1324291015

424497BV00001B/1/P